KARL PETERSEN

URBAN FITS

To Leah —
Companions on the
journey!

Karl

destinēe

destinēe

Published by Destinée Media., www.destineemedia.com
Book formatting by Per-Ole Lind
Cover design by Douglas Winter
All rights reserved by the author.

ISBN 978-0-9759082-9-7

TABLE OF CONTENTS

I

II

III

IV

I

Pigeon Matins

angels rapt in a flurry
are gathering in a blur
of dream and wakefulness,
interposing pigeons' coos,
morning canticles

passing wings
grace the window pane

at the parting of curtains
the angels arise
in a tidy choir on wires,
mumble matins—
a summons drawing me
from dormancy
down the telephone lines
through a huddle of hemlocks
and beyond
to the powers that be

Commencement for an Urban Poet

Feed in gutters and limos,
feed on the disenfranchised,
or the franchised
in their penthouse suites
with crisp as lettuce
clean smelling suits,
silk ties.

Like mangy strays, scavenge
on unsuspecting passersby
toting shopping bags
of rage and grief
of love lost or told off or never found.
Dig for naive harmonies
playing in a boy's hands beneath
sweet-smelling hair, beneath
the coat of demure, pubescent grins
against the bus stop wall.

Like mice, poke
at spent shells uncovered
in musty corners
of stair wells
in East Hastings hotels,
press until
shells break with light
from junkies' sleepless nights
and labyrinthine dreams.

Then, like hawks swoop,
fondle in tall grass swaying
with hushed jubilation;
soar azure heavens
and claw at the pre-dawn sky
until it bleeds redemption
from a star-struck dew drop
clinging to the sleeve of night.

Moochers

"Lord, even the dogs under the table
eat the children's crumbs." (Mark 7:28)

The gulls Sunday morning
scream up the alley outside church,
diving and pillaging dumpsters,
gleaning on last night's revelries.

They plead
down the corridors
of our sleepy prayers,
drop and genuflect
for the mass of loosed excess,
clamor for still more
with each turn

until as one
the ragtag beats it down
Broadway and up
over the bars, the dress shops
and darkened banks, rejoicing
over a slice of Wonder bread
that waves like an ensign
in the lead bird's beak.
He'll be breaking it
without ceremony
among the band.

What Latte Said to Honey

Come to me, Sweet,
twist on the torso of my spoon
and smoothly
woo me with your harmonies.
Dip in, turn, toss me over
again, and over,
swirl in this girl's milky ways.
And when we are one

let us go to that one there
sitting alone, smiling in our afterglow
as he sips the sweet elixir of us
to his froth-crested lips,
into the very veins, ah! with sighs
to the mellow strains
of "Honey and Latte."

Executing Things

The meshing flesh to flesh comes easily
but the marriage will require execution. We sigh
at our gathered parts uneasy with the merger—
boxes teetering ceiling high, books leaning,
displaced and mystified, waiting assignments. Talc
deliberates with deodorant over the right drawers,
right armpits. Left on the counter, mugs vie with plates,
even jarred pickles are begging for elbowroom,
for some relief, please, from this insistent stuffing in,
fitting ribs into the clefts of another, pimple to dimple,
and bending torsos round, unfitting for conjugal bliss.

Somberly, the execution begins—
my foot rest goes, my floor lamp half standing
after serving many nights' reading, her palm tree
(but a palm can survive anything, she pleads,
she knows, even weeks of neglect in a corner) all
off to Sally Ann, as well as the suit I've saved for events
I never attend. My Hugo painting of the fat lady
picking lavender (she calls Butt Ugly) just won't go
so it must go. Her plastic Christmas wreath, my crèche
with a severed shepherd's head and a lamb shank gone,
my several re-severed candles—all executed,
into the ally dumpster. My decomposing high school
letter jacket is spared, I worked hard for that. Her lamp
stays, and I only hope it serves books well. Her
bamboo ladder (rescued from the dumpster) also lives
rising from the hearth to a dead end at the ceiling,
a reminder about holding to unrealistic dreams.

We compare mental checklists
of the condemned and the saved, bicker and cry,
stare at the bedroom walls. They hold us like a pledge.
Silence trembles after the parsing and purging
as we feel a greater death running beneath us
and all things, like a steady stream—the slow
sloughing off of "selves for self's sole sake"—
a good death that will spare no scarcity to spare us,
will declare bankruptcy for the merger of souls.

Visions Hunt the Lonely Down

From his window at work with a sandwich,
thinking no one is noticing him,
he looks down on a sun soaked plaza
where folks retiring from offices
sit in suits and hunch over carryout lunches.
A student sprawls in baggy pants
like a crime scene chalk outline.

One woman in a string strap dress
whips back a strand of brown hair
over a shoulder and pauses
catching his look from above, their eyes
link by a thread of light like
the Blessed Mary to the strange intruder;
she waits, pondering this to herself:
life-altering propositions are born
in the upward cast of an eye.

Mementos

at moments a Kitsilano loneliness
invokes patterns in a sunlit café

saxophone riffs from Charlie Parker
ebb over the dull din

a fleeting shadow
of hair and shoulders flickers past

breaking the concentration of table light
and reminiscences of absence

Cliché Like a Lance

Every morning
I'm sent the same cliché—
a spring sparrow singing
from the fence post
in the back garden,
some saccharine old tune
about "love in spite of you."

Its theme like wool pajamas
chafes a boil on my chest
saturated with the puss of bad dreams:
tangled vines, dog fights,
and picket fences, slow rain,
and pools of spite and us.

There, the sparrow's trill again
penetrates the thicket
lancing old wounds
that trickle like practicing scales
for a summer overture
in an overturned garden.

Fossett Flies Solo Around the World

Our go-it-aloneness
and our phrases praise us,
accolades to ourselves
ring the skies:
we have *conquered space,*
made one giant leap,
gained air superiority,
broken barriers
of sound, of time
and atmosphere.
These thoughts propel us
everywhere
but to the heavens.

September 11

Morning of 9/11, the T.V. is left on for me,
the sound off. My roommates I guess
wanted me to see this: the clear, stark images,
without words, as it is for them in New York.

In dawn light the 1+1 of the Twin Towers
is not adding up, conjoined twins
in an hour of incongruous thought: a flaw,
an odd ball billows

on the building's side like a cancer,
concocting monsters out of sublimity.
Then a sudden burst of red and yellow.
(Did they say flight 11?) One monolith

implodes, descends in a cloud,
erasing story upon story
upon untold stories of sons, mothers
and husbands, families unfolding,

sending out the hollow calls on 9-1-1.
New York's double child, the darling hubris
turned to debris among shards, leaving
a scaffold of crooked crosses,

eerily conjuring Charles Manson's love
of Revelation 9-11 and *Exterminus*
and the four angels from the pit.
9-1-1 flashes in everything sudden

penetrating fragile sleep as commercial jets
fly over the houses louder than before
on landing paths into Vancouver International,
begging questions of *What if...?*

Navigating the Dawn

The thought
of how a baby navigates
the pre-dawn of its birth—
twisting and somersaulting
like an astronaut
in a cramped capsule
eager to stretch his legs
in outer space
as the amniotic dance
pushes him for glory,
the sound of God
a heartbeat away
(urging him on)
until he's finally out there
hanging on a corkscrew lifeline
to the mother ship—
is not a thought
we usually go to the office with,

though we've all been there
restless to escape
the comfort
of watery solitudes
for exotic constellations

as we rumble and bump along
in this tin womb of a bus
doing the transit dance
heading out
all jumbled together
glum and waiting for the sun to rise

becoming pregnant
in the wet deep of December
with poignant thoughts of
how babies navigate the dawn.

Unattended Relief

On the way to the every day job in grey
success snakes slickly down the road. Drowning in
the monotonous wet hiss, I do not notice

the strands of the new overpass looping away
to dead split ends. I've never taken note of how
the bridge sniffs up lines of workers in their cars

to maintain the corporate rush. A fresh
sun cannot lift my eyes to the line of mountains
starkly inscribing the ancestors' old stories
above the floors of Vancouver's towers. Less do I see

the rare relief on a sun-drenched barn
and how this goes unattended, its board face
mirroring the land's stressed furrows. Nor do I see

my salvation in the shimmering bridge cables,
how they quiver with a baptized glory, knowing
the harsh mercy in their corroding loose holds.

Getting Wired at the Monk

At the Wired Monk, we're the beautiful people
dragging in Monday morning not so beautiful,
espresso screaming for a homerun in the veins.

Junkies fall into queue, roll up their sleeves
for a caffeine line straight to the heart, shift
left and right, as the milky hiss cajoles and teases.

No other love will do, devotion's end
and this her temple, where conflicts come
resolved, where unrealized dreams revolve.

Spiritual Discipline

"a time for everything under the sun"

Once a week
on the morning ride downtown,
we get a lesson on time management:

       the bus door opens,
       five blocks from work
       and forty beyond home,
       where waiting on the pavement,
       not entering, stands
       the leather-jacketed Jesus freak
       at full-bus volume
       rattling off his sermon for the day
       (sometimes a prayer)
       in the thirty seconds
       it takes riders to file on
       and the door to quickly close.

This is for irritated bus drivers,
embarrassed businessmen,
and bemused office clerks

just in case we forget
the time and distance between
work and home,
sin and forgiveness,
emptiness and bread.

II

Opening Blinds At the Cathedral

a communion wafer
snaps bone white
in the priest's hands

the gift of God for the people of God

his lapel mike
shatters the sanctuary air

a baby cackles

for a split second

waking the hearts
of the worry-weighted

and cracking the blinds
of a high rise cubicle

The Price You Pay

The problem with poetry is it costs so much.
You pay for more than just the words
(10% for the writer's migraine medication)
and the cover (20% for the publisher).
You also pay for the paper (70% for the lumber
companies) much of it unused mulch

as
empty space

on the page

     and in the forest

                on the mountainsides

       like a vast paper desert

...for just pausing

a sigh

                                                                and

silent wondering

about the value of a poem

and what it costs you.

Word, Become Flesh

A little scared, you say, to go
face to face—our voices unfiltered
would be too much. You prefer
the screen of written words
draping our computers
three hundred k away

while finger tips tease,
conjure intimacy from keyboards.

Our bodies, pixels clustered and
pickled in picture files, fear salvation.
Shared flesh might intrude
on our favorite ghosts and nightmares.

You'd prefer the forfeiture
of a God-born image, not risk
the possibility of corporeal entity
should fingers stop their tapping
and entwine like quicksilver,

should eyes dance naked
with strange warmth
as they take in the whole of us,

and our lips part, grasping
the breadth of a sudden sunrise
in our eyes, press out fear
with a horizon-wide embrace.

Smokin' Jesus

I.

Jesus used to smoke a cigar at the bagel joint
sorta lonely and tired lookin' out
from the stained glass window by the front door
where he always perched.
But he just disappeared one day,
kicked out, the manager said,
on account of patron's complaints,
some anti-smokers, some religious fanatics.

So why am I so down then?
I guess I should feel good
if they're cleaning out the place of free-loaders
nabbing the smokin' Jesus in stained glass
instead of me.

Could be that I'm the next to go though,
cuz I've been scammin' refill after refill
on my dollar seventy-five for a regular,
and I've been wearin' out my chair
for sixty-five pages of Flannery O'Conner,
while the big spenders stand waitin' for a seat,
their mochas and Mexi-bagels in hand.

Come to think of it,
Jesus' smoke never bothered me,
broken up in the window like a kaleidoscope
bleedin' every color of the rainbow.

Kinda gave me comfort in fact, and someone
to talk to,
like that day I just got back from Japan and
couldn't understand where all the people had gone,
or that rainy Monday night
after my ma died some three thousand miles away
and nobody here who understood, nobody
but Jesus at the bagel joint, that is,
smokin' a stogie in stained glass.

II.

Jesus came back again
the other day at the bagel joint
when nobody was looking.
He's sitting at his same old perch
in the window by the door, his stogie balanced
between two fingers in his right hand,
watching the patrons file in:
a woman in green beret
and black tights followed by a business suit and tie,
both alone,
a covey of girl teens in hip-hugger jeans
and belly buttons peeping about
ogling boys who swagger in
with their pants half-way to their knees,
a woman in blue sequined hair
not quite sure where she is
on the arm of a long-white-bearded man
and worn leather satchel, looking a bit
like Jesus himself.

Espresso is screaming from behind the counter
and bagel smells jump the queue—
toasted and creamed in cheese and lox;

the youthful protestations, too, of unfaithful love
(or was it just a dirty joke?)

the strung out in the corner,
weighted with the memories of abandoned friends
spilling out onto the table,
making the candle flame quiver
as her fingers swipe across jaundiced cheeks;

the belly laughs of three guys
regurgitating last night's sordid memories
filled with innuendo and vain wishes;

The sequined hair stares
with a starry late-night gaze
past the bearded man
through the stain glass where Jesus sits,
and into eternity, and beyond,
as if she sees something no one else can
except Jesus, who's hanging out incognito
in broken pieces of green, purple and apple glass,
just smokin' a stogie
and trying to take it all in.

Wrong Bus

Bus #9 cuts jagged across Kitsilano.
Doors fold open, slam shut,
take in and spit out: office personnel,
grandmothers with wire baskets on wheels,
and a school girl on the highway to success,
trying to pocket a degree before her last bus ride,
though little does she know about street urchins
on another trip to loose change.

Like the odd kid in polyester pants
and thick black-rimmed spectacles
on his third thrill ride of the day
talking up the driver at eight decibels
about the way the windshield wipers
slap across the windows, thwak, thwak,
and how maybe he ought to get them fixed
before they fall off.

The bus with its gut load
listens on in titters as the driver
tries to exercise BC Transit cordiality
and keep an eye on the traffic.

A thin old man creeps up between
the driver and the polyester kid with a request:
"Where's Butt? I need Butt."

Before the driver can draw a breath,
polyester pants leaps in to assist:
"Butt? You wanna be on Davie Street.
Oh, Butte! Driver, I think he wants Butte.
You want Butte?" at nine decibels now.
Polyester pants, he knows the lay of the land.

"Butte," the old man, strained and scratchy,
implores the driver.
.

But before the driver can speak,
polyester chimes, "You ain't anywhere
near Butte! Butte's across the bridge! Get off
here and change to #22. Right here, get off!"

The thin old man side-steps off,
seeking a last word of affirmation from the driver:
"Boot this way?"

"It's not Boot, it's Butte!" Polyester roars,
turning again to his confidant behind the wheel.
"I wonder what medication he's on, eh?"

Stripping

Guitar man without a home
busks on West Broadway every Thursday
doling out street-wise pearls
to the lingerie lady
who steps high heeled out the shop door
to check her front window display.
He's singing,
So hide a couple dollars
In the bottom o' your cup
'cuz the drought'll come,
yeah, it'll come some day
an' strip you right down
till there's nothin' left
but skin and bone.
Glimpsing him over her shoulder
she ducks red-faced inside
undressed by his lonesome dirge,
by his blood shot eyes, dreary words
of her empty cups and deserted home.

Lunatics

People with cell phones think nothing
of going about in public
waving their arms and turning pirouettes,
sometimes laughing as in an empty room,
and talking to no one elemental,

street lunatics, only much worse.
At least the ones who pan for coin
don't insist on Aldo shoes and Raybans,
and at least they make
I-contact-with-you
and ask you for a cigarette.

Fashion Angel of Robson Street

Feel, can you, though you
stand frozen on that pedestal?
Draped and re-draped
in the finest lingerie
with the turning of seasons
for the high rollers creasing easy cash
and gawking through store front glass?

Feel, can you,
the seductive set-up, the tease?
The way they tear you down
and take you for a ride
naked on your back now
aboard a clangy hand dolly
through the downtown corridors,
through intersections of the city grind
and the grime of opaque high rise air?

Smell it, hear the giggles
of your entourage, the mockeries,
as they see you stripped down
to plastic flesh.

And see, can you, what no else can
gazing up from glazed wide eyes into a sky
you have longed for
like the arms of a stranger?

You charm and alarm,
reluctant Fashion Angel,
with your impenetrable eyes,
your ghostly halo of synthetic red hair,
your shiny plastic arm with no hand
out-stretched in perpetual supplication.

Bacchus

There may be nothing more sublime
than finding
beneath the window of Bacchus Botique
  with its displays of silk suits
  300-dollar hand bags
  creamy lace gowns enigmatically
  hung over headless busts
  and torsos cut off at the knees
  pale pink plastic necks smooth
  like the attendees gliding the floor
  with chins high
  and refined mystic smiles

nothing more oblique or eloquent perhaps
than finding on your side of the window
a perfectly formed dog doo:
cylindrical and neatly cropped
nut-brown as a Bahama tan
and freckled kindly in corn niblets
attempting obscurity.

Secretly you wish you'd thought of doing that,
and you remember with a smile
your mother's word
for whenever you went
pee-pee or poo outside: *bacchus*!

Morning Mass

Take it in—
the mile long dawn, bumper to bumper
on the downtown commute,
cutting through the heart
of forests of firs of yesteryears
lying a century under the cemetery
of a city planner's asphalt draft,
compassed and parceled out in street grids
that carry our race in its diurnal pace.
See how the houses hold up their shingles of cedar
like wafers of penitence? (This is our due.)

Drink it in—
brake lights stalling you
in a memory that nags from last night's quarrel,
bumpers snarling— your daily wine.
You can only wait and curse and cry for mercy.

Watch now, your priest ap-
pears. On a nearby chimney,
an orphan squirrel of bygone wood groves, survivor,
raises little hands to offer up your absolution—
how quickly and nimbly
he negotiates your labyrinth of guilt,
dashing over the housetops with deft invocations
in the twitches of his tail, into a tree,
onto the expressway of telephone cables
that scurries him over the Granville gridlock
like an arrow prayer at morning mass.
Then he is gone again, into a confessional of firs.

N/A

The guy in the black Benz
at the full serve pump
got me fired cuz he told the boss I
pumped him five dollars
and three cents
when he asked for only five.
The boss calls and wakes me up
the next morning.

Where are you?

     I'm fired.

No you're not, get your ass in here.

     You said I'm fired,
     so I'm taking the day off.

The hell you are, and if you don't get in here
I'll really fire you.

I go in.

See this? It's your application form.
He throws it down on the Shell logo
that blazes across the counter,
beer on his breath.

     I already filled it out.

I know ya did. I sent it to headquarters,
and they sent it back.

What for?

See all those N/A's? You put 'em
in all these empty blanks here where
you haven't worked or anything.
They said it's perfect.

It is?

They said nobody's ever done that right before.
They wanna use this for an example
from our station
to show people not to leave anything blank
no matter what you haven't done.

Really? Do I get anything for that?

Yeah, you get to keep your job.
Get your ass out there.

The gas bell dings twice
and there's the guy in the black Benz again
at the full serve.
He struts over pulling at his belt.

Five fifty. Not a cent more or less.

Dance, Devil, Dance

cite statistics of gun deaths
in the U.S.
just to make you feel good again
that we're not them,
then lean back for another swig
of Canadian
and turn on the hockey game—
cross check, high stick, spear
and the gloves come off

dance Devil, dance, oh yeah
havin' a good time now

order out for sushi
and make out with the Persian chick,
and the next day Latino,
just to let your friends know
you're cool, you're hip, ya know,
cuz you're a global activist too

dance, Devil, dance
havin' a good time now

change the diaper on the baby
without a word, so cool,
because your saccharin smile says it all:
see me? I'm a new age sensitive guy cuz
I'm doing the jelly fish dance for the kid,
now where's the chicks
bring 'em on, oh yeah

dance, Devil, dance
havin' a good time now
listen over the table
to the guy who's tellin' you
God sucks, He's dead, bang
as you nod appreciatively,
oh yeah,
to show your sensitivity

dance, Devil, dance
havin' a good time now

then Sunday morning
at the back of the church
make an announcement:
Satan's changed his mind
and wants to say he's sorry
so let's all just say a prayer right now
and ask God to forgive him
oh yeah

dance, Devil, dance down the aisles
you're havin' a good time now

Canadian Rockwell

If Norman Rockwell had painted Vancouver,
he'd have done a corner in my neighborhood
and painted the name Wong
across a convenience store façade,
and he'd have painted in a street urchin
with blonde locks falling from a fall knit cap
dashing across our picture
from Wong's, left to right, shoeless,
candy bars spilling from vest pockets
with Wong behind intercepting her
mid-intersection.

Vancouver corner still-framed,
our own Canadian Rockwell.

And we're there too, the ad hoc jury,
in our hikers, gortex, leather coats
and brown leather purses,
babies in their luxury coupe buggies
at the 4-way stop, all posed,
rubber-necking and wide-eyed
to the focal point.

When we fast forward
to the next portrait in the series,
the cops are cuffing the waif, propped
disheveled and drug-induced
against a lamp post by Wong's,
her yellow maw frozen in a scream
while Wang recovers candy bars
from the pavement. We, the onlookers,
are turning away as rain descends,
some pulling up hoods, covering baby,
and cavorting over lat night's hockey game
with an air of good losers.

Korean Litter

Waiting for the number ten
she suddenly points
to a piece of wrinkled wrapper
lying alone on the pavement
at the bus stop.
She erupts with delight,
the first words she's uttered all night,
"Look, Korean litter!"

Sure enough,
Bowl Soup, it says,
Made in Korea, lunch
for a Granville Street waif,
perhaps, or just a little
home comfort for this girl
having blown here to a stop,
one long ocean away.

Those Who Have Not Must Cling

In the oldest part of town,
like jilted lovers bereft of sense of self
we clutch to
a rare vestige of our history:

reaching from the pavement,
four steel girders hold up an 1890's brick façade,
like a head stone,
brittle as a eulogy.

Through the façade's gaps and portals,
those who take pause
see backhoes
clawing out holes for new foundations,

and beyond the façade, upward,
see clouds
passing like reluctant spirits
from tombs of a fragile ancestry.

Indulgences

A songbook he thought I wanted
rests neatly by my reading lamp,
a fresh pot of coffee and Haagen-Dazs,
all etched with overtures—
penance or forgiveness, who knows—
     Hello, how was your day?
     There's leftover lasagna,
     have some tea.
counter tops wiped like empty bar
on a fresh score.

So we stack the shelves
of our encounters
even more precariously
with indulgences,
tumble in the clefs
of our dissonant conversations
with even louder undertones.

In every glance vibrations
run up the nerve strands, plucked
like two strings out of tune.

The Problem with Pickles

If there's room, we try to cram it full—
but the problem with pickles is space.
To find a larger jar seems the answer,
but a second thought proves the case

that a pickle's prone to gathering
others in kind, each assigned a place,
maximizing for high density living.
It's all one rabid, tenacious race

to have our homes and eat them too,
stuff them with toys, trim and lace,
not a step lost in the consumption
of the world's things for things sakes.

More room begs more pickles still, you see,
especially dill. So to keep the pace
we can't cut back and live with less
or simply abide with a smaller place—

that's a sacred scarcity scarce few can stand,
for with the purging of pickles we face
the craving, a lust for more, til' we burn
or the hunger burns, consumed by grace.

Christmas Beggars

umbrellas may negotiate Christmas
but they fail to protect
against the isolating chill

men as candles will stoop unlit at bus stops
begging for the kindling of fires
with disowning kin

the thrum-hiss of a passing bus full
drowns out wet cell phones on cheeks
peppermint lattes do not console

we beckon connections not transmittable
through wireless pleasantries
pressed to lips and ears

no amount of holiday good will will fulfill
like a warm reception
of the message flesh to flesh

The Child Seer Takes a Portrait

The child sees all
that matters and knows
without being told, she knows
with her questions—

> *Why did you come for Christmas,*
> *are you all by yourself?*

as only a child can,
without embarrassment
at improprieties with guests
or holiday decorum,
> *Why doesn't anyone want you?*

simply gazing in
through the frosted, half-lit
window of your eyes—
> *You need to have some fun.*

She rends the matter of the heart
transparent
with renderings as sweet
as snow curling over eaves,
as uncompromising
as the flick of a camera shutter
on Christmas Eve

III

Crow Vespers

crows congregating
buoyed on last light
fly watch over hamlets
braiding threads of
chimney smoke upward
like unwitting prayers
the Spirit prays for us
whispered in petitions
of the grief and fears
of the vicissitudes
of night and morrow

Since September 11

Since September 11
I always face the door
and eat more and
don't stay in the basement long.

I believe more in play
and work, how I
mark an essay—a comma, like a sigh,
bears the weight of a world's waiting.

I care now
how I walk the golf course
and with whom,
care less about who wins the world series
(though the Yankees seem a fitting end)
care more about the game.

Also think of old friends often and
high school, and even go back down
through the two hour border check
to see if it's all still there—the school,
the football bleachers, the guys—they are,
and glad to see the old dog again, I even
get a hug. But the small
town cheer is gone,
the intoxicating buzz of homecoming,
the color washed
from the town's pallid eyes
and I do not know
whose eyes have changed,
theirs or mine.

Today at the mall I noticed
water trickling from a fountain
brittle as baby's breath
while a flute played
"All things bright and beautiful"
and heard trembling instead of tremolo.
At a shop I stopped at a door,
one like my mom's linen closet
back at the old house in Platte,
and just stared
until a clerk tapped my shoulder.
In the change room area a door
creaked and groaned
like the iron gate back home,
so I opened it again,
and again,
just to let old times in
(Dad's suspender pants
and wing-tipped shoes)
just to stop the changing inside.

In the underground garage my eyes
locked with a complete stranger's.
We talked across the hollow about nothing
to fill the void with voice
with the empty words of our
out of place commiseration,
as if believing this, this could last
until we neither feared nor wanted,
nor wanted to go our separate ways.

Return to Youth on a Drive Home

A West Coast pace at 2 PM post-work
will set your heart rate to low
on the road to regression.

It's perhaps the way the highway
shuttles you from the Surrey sprawl
through the monoliths on Alex Fraser Bridge,
then sweeps you—right, left—
on yawning arcs along the river,
which spreads arms lethargically west
after a day of treacherous falls, rocky negotiations,
or how suddenly a scent of fresh cow dung
wraps around the windshield,
or the way a field of hay lays
sweetly down, sweeping you back
for a taste of grandpa's farm.

On Vancouver's south side warehouses flicker by
like frames of old film footage tripping off the tongue—
Yamato, Nintendo, We Shop Costco.

You regress because of the way
Blenheim Street maples
leaf down as a coronation row
to you the youthful prince
as sun flecks through with laurels of light
until you are not driving but flying
as the child once did
with school on hold and
the only books cracked
were the fantasies you opened
with the wood screen door's

springy twang! clap!
prologue to eternity of days
in sudden sun gushes
after-rain puddles
sneakers and lapping dogs
mother's chidings fading behind
from the welcomed solace
of an empty house.

The rhythmic k-thunk, k-thunk,
of tires on King Edward
is your homeward mantra,
slowing you enough to catch
the call of robins from the brush
on the back stretch through Kitsilano.

Under a blooming cherry
you look up, pink on baby blue,
into a upturned bowl of candy,
picking and savoring your way
through the branches
and beyond the tasty elements
to your final regression.

Evening Portrait

Without warning you might
suddenly see yourself
unfolded across the evening sky—

sun-dyed anxiety stretched threadbare
in thin vermilion wisps of cloud,
bruised blotches of ochre
on a drenched sheet of blue
as cruel words thrum still
with a shrill timbre in the heart.
Red rage flares
at the extremities of wounds,
waiting for the numbing of night.

And then with the spilling
of the paint wells
into this gaudy span of sky
you may suddenly go giddy,
dripping tinged tears
like a helpless fool in color
while you watch the spent
paint-smeared artist himself
get brushed in as well.

Crayon City

As kids we drew the cityscape
as a crayon collage of heads,
eyes, noses, and mouths
like a simple prophetic truth:

Downtown is the face of us
with shiny make-up, tucks,
suctions and made over places.
Pits, moles, and deep scars
appeared in our crayon cities
where Magenta loitered
on the corner twitching,
or Midnight Blue lingered
in an anonymous window,
or Forest Green went
over the line with Dandelion.

And today when work is done
we pour from downtown
like over-used, frazzled crayons
frenetic for home, bawling
with faint rejoicing, toting
our precious city-creations
along with our abscesses and
ulcers and more absences to fill
with whatever color we find.

The Man on the Inside

Today the God Van sits on Granville
with the sky dropping drapes of rain beads
down its windshield finger-painted white
with the assurance: "God brings clarity."

The long-haired man inside,
his chimera eyes dancing with self-possession
like a street-side apparition, gapes
through his windshield's streams of beads.

The passersby squint
with a moment's recognition, then
on their ways they run impatiently
to other recurring dreams.

Late October Footfall

Tennis shoes
        sink in
                a thawing lawn
                        as geese call
                                vee-ing across
                                        a muted west—
                                beckoning back to
                        recollect
                streams and
        abandoned
        wellsprings.

Benediction

He glides the streets
with random cordiality
pulling the black hood of his sweatshirt up
against a February drizzle.

Outside a coffee shop
he stops at the nearest table,
tells his mutt *down*
and leans back against the window.

He spots his next audience
in a young woman caressing
a latte against one cheek.
She glances his way.

Yes, that's the look he looks for,
the one he knows too well—
dislocation and want—
and reaching beneath his covers somewhere
he pulls a bottle out,
takes a swig herky-jerky and smiles,
magnanimous gaps in his teeth:
>   *wonderful isn't it, the rain,*
>   *it just never stops,*
>   *you can't get this anywhere out east.*

He sends up a sudden gush of good will
in a tongue that only angels comprehend
as he extends his arms wide to the street
to enfold the day—
the tires hissing by,
the soporific milky-gray,
taking them all in
to where he aches.

As she half stands to slide away
in mid-benediction, he darts his hand
out to hers, which she ignores.
So he calls his mutt and runs,
leaving his arms wide there as an outline
in the mist of the coffee shop window.

History Thundering in a Culvert

In towns as these
cradled maternally
by mountain and sea,

you want to remember nothing
of the sordid sad stories you left behind—
overseas, back east, down south—
to know nothing
but the blissful, immeasurable now.

Your history once renounced
eventually re-announces itself in sweaty sleeps,
in light trickle of water through a gully
along a dark hillside, or along a logging road:
silent grief
gathering and seeping
as threads of rain
for the downward cause.
Its import can only be caught
in the intersections
of time, space, and grace.

On a street-damp evening
at a corner in Kitsilano
a lamp light stops you to recall it.
Beneath the sheen of the cookie lid of a manhole
grieving resounds in a hollow rush—
cycle of sea, wormwood skies, petulant rain.
Uncovered, the culvert could open up
not a wonderland
but a wondering of lands forgotten.

Your history as a culvert thunders under you,
recollecting your wanderings
like a life-long friend's steady shaping of you
by gathering streams,
like the drawing of blood to the heart.

Battle for Jeremiah's Air Waves

At Jeremiah's the sound system's bawling
Pumpkin Heads. The bartender and patrons
spar lame one-liners across the pub
on the subject of sexual escapades.

They're speculating stocks one table over,
at another a baseball team's
barking its preferred means of inebriation.
And across from me my friend

explains in the din, exaggerating gestures,
the intricacies of the little stethoscopes
that receive sound in the hypothalamus
of the brains he's been studying and how

the neurons can distinguish between
significant signals and static. I congratulate him
significantly, asking how the neurons know
which voices to listen to and which to ignore.

Bulimic Season

What she sees is the cyclic churn:
the after-summer flurry of chestnuts
and a premature de-leafing
tossed onto an oily pavement,
and the umber violence
under the steady hiss of wet tires.

She sees nights bleeding slowly into days
without horizons, and nightmares

of chestnut leaf puree in the streets,
washing down gutters and gullets
into the city's charted belly,
churning ocean-side through
corrugated aluminum mouths.
She sees only this endless ritual, this
throwing all to the deadpan bay.

He Heard, She Heard

The band plays,
drowning out all sound
but the fantasies in their heads.

He turns on his stool
with a little shimmy
of his shoulders
to the beat,
unwittingly
catching the eye of the girl
in knee-length summer dress
with string straps.
She takes his look
as an invitation and pulls up
a stool. A finger
goes up the sweaty side of her glass
and caresses the crevice
at the base of her neck.

Actually, I wasn't looking at you, he says,
I was just watching the band.
Through the din she hears:
 I was looking at you.
That watch goes with your hand.

Thank you, she says, *it's gold-plated.*

Go dating? We just met. Really,
I just want to hear the band.

She hears *hand*, so she extends it
with the gold watch,
like she wants him to kiss it,
but he just holds it, then shakes it once.
I'm Darren, he says.

> *Oh* are *you? I'm daring too, with the right guy.*

You're Darren, too? I don't believe you.

> *Just watch and you'll see.*

Your watch? Yeah, fancy, but I'm not—

> *Watch me dance? Sure.*

Really, I just came to hear the music.

> She pulls him by the hand
> and leads him to the floor,
> he tries to dance.

> *Did you come here alone?* she asks.

*No, I don't own a home. What are
you, a real estate agent?*

> *What?*

I live in a basement. I really don't want to dance.

Embarrassment? About dancing? Why?

Because it's better than living with my parents.

Your pants are fine. Don't worry about it.

But... you've never met them. They're awful.

Your butt looks fine in them.
What? Are they too tight?

Yeah, they're up tight. Never liked me
going out to places like this.

You feel like going out? When?

All the time. I got sick of it so I had to leave.

You have to leave?
Would you like some company?

You own a company?

Sure, why don't I join you?

Thanks, I could use the work. Could I take your number?

What?

Your phone number, he shouts.

Sure. Here's my card. But---

Great. We'll talk sometime.

The Sound of Feet Dragging

The moon plays hide-and-seek
between roof-tops,
sandals on the walkway
drag out this long leave-taking.

They whisper wistful regrets, assurances
of rendezvous, knowing full well
these promises can only float
for the moment in a balmy night
while cares are sloughing off.

Promises like these
evaporate in a city like this
soon after the two have parted
east and west,
after the scuff of sandals
is swallowed by the light of day,
after one look at the list
of tasks undone,
items not bought,
deadlines,
accumulated notes re: notes,
paths not run.

Foreplay

summer surrenders
to late September greys
over English Bay

though even the mist
for all its sullen self-pity
breaks for this

a great
    rainbow
        arc
          of
            love
    remembered
pours down
a foreplay of harvest

vibrant light
kisses down the spine
of hills and supine parks

after a season of postponements
and delayed satisfactions

as gulls transcend
in laughter
elated with the anticipation
of promises to fulfill

Faithful Ones

The Christmas carnival midway is closing down,
while the Great Light of the east runs its course,

trailing in its wake clouds of pink cotton
that catch on December's late boughs;

Boxing Day winds frenetic paths down Broadway:
one acolyte fingers loose change in his pocket

and peers lustily through the shop window
at Nikon cameras knocked down fifty bucks;

another staggers under the spoils of the scavenging
as she scrambles a hasty exit out the front door;

the merry-makers, for now, still have Christmas
by the balls, bells, bows and won't let go; shop doors

swing and ring, and even facades tenaciously cling
to their spray can snow and Christmas embroidery.

Leaving a Family Holiday

At departure gate 2
perfunctory hugs around
a circling of sibs
embrace a family history
written in the gestures
and platitudes.

> *Great havin' ya*

> > *Yep. So ... Gotta git goin'. Our plane ...*

> *Yep, and we gotta git back. Car
> parked on $3 an hour ya know.*

> > *Git out my way sometime
> > why doncha?*

> *Sure, you betcha.*

And little sister's voice
like a bell tower in hollow chests
chimes,

> *You want us to git out of your way?*

and chuckles buckle down the line of passengers
like Dominos and Backgammon and Risk,
passengers who know as much as we
about the ambiguities
of family holiday good-byes.

I Will Sup With Him

August spreads cream and yellow cloud scraps
across a summer-stretched dusk—

potato peels left on God's table after
the day's turning, unearthing, and paring.

This recalls late afternoons when I was ten,
drops of sun trickling down our brown necks

as you pushed with canvas shoes on the spade
and I knelt above the splitting ground

waiting for the cold, rough nuggets
to erupt like gold from dark caverns.

In the kitchen you slipped a knife
into the slick spud-white flesh,

with deft strokes, the snap,
you split our toil into boiling pots

while my boy's hands swam
in a Formica top of potato skins

fumbling with all God's glory,
lost in sums and fractions of sky.

IV

Resurrection

on a Cascade ridge
hushed under
a November crescent

a deafening mist
enfolds
amplifying the lungs

dark wings
on an updraft
ascend
the hollow
of your central chambers
into a vaporous canopy

the raven's guttural call
so laden
so utter
with ancient truth

rattles
the deadwood
vaulted
in a yawning rib cage

Unclogging Arteries

I always like this movement,
she says, on Oak Street
as we head out of town—
the traffic thins, arteries unclog,

leaving a steady diet of urban hubris—
the downsizing, upgrading, supersizing.

We feel the flow now, the sweet
rush of unhurried anticipation,
easing down to a right lane pace,
a Corinne Bailey Rae tune
modulating the heart. Her hand
lays out an offering across my lap—
relinquishment and replenishment,
the us in the now.

Our heads go giddy with escape, caught
in the blessed bliss of delinquency,
as we cross the wood bridge to the delta,
re-immerse in Eden.

Open car windows usher in strait scents—
sea and glade dance over the rim of the marsh.
We trap deep draughts in the lungs,
concentrate remission there,
clearing our city-glutted veins
and pathways for the play of gyrfalcons
and muskrats, mallards and sand hill cranes.

At the sanctuary we trace junkos
up trellising limbs, then rise
in the slow wave of snow geese, fodder-full.
White folds over blue.
We find our pitch in the flocking crescendo
as they lift us beyond the horizon
to a forgotten country where we
are fed and feted with airs
in vast unsullied flyways.

Anomaly

We commiserated over
the carnivorous stranger out back,
as to her name, her make,
surely not from these parts,

her rare plumage bright, resplendent
in mid-January sun
on the cold limbs of the cherry tree,
resting so close, within our grasp.

Kestrel?   no, too large
Goshawk?   too small I think
Sharp-shinned?
     we peruse the guide books
     like travelers in a new city
     of color, habit and song
Pigeon hawk?
     book says they're in open country
     and winter in the gulf states
     (tell that to the bird
     she never read the book)
Male or female?
     female, for sure, see, it's more drab
Falcon, accipiter or buteo?
     I dunno,
     haven't seen it move
     for the last hour n' a half

Elusive beauty
perching too proudly
for ease of acquaintance,
speak your name,
your smooth overtures beguiling
in the curve of your beak,
the impassive, distant eyes.

We turn from the patio view,
from her worship Cleopatra
on her cherry throne
mocking our impotence

and glance back once more,
but she is gone like the germ of a poem.

Just a spot-lit moment
of dumbfounded
winter-spun wondering.

On the Backs of White Mares

Your feet on a pebbled road
fall amplified with each step,
and you feel the first sliding away:
the ferry easing back from the landing,
a long sigh fading in the wake.

The island woo's so furtively
you hardly notice how quickly
the city's anesthetic wears off
down the shore, but even then you fear
it may not be real, that this may be just
a clever technique to wrest the soul
from urban moorings and the city-tides
sedating ebbs and flows—
waking, work, and walking weary home—
perhaps a fantasy setting you up
before the double-cross back to there.

But with another step
you are re-sensitized: the soundless woods,
a shed, a crow, appear to be eyeing you,
the odd long-awaited guest.
There the cottage perches story-book-like
on the meadow's crest,
and you think again that it could be
a cup of capricious grace sent to dupe,
but you keep drinking it in anyway

as you feel the second sliding away while
easing down under the full-bloomed cherry.
And now it is raining white mares on you,

and closing your eyes you are
suddenly riding, a gulf breeze in your face,
down a pastured slope, over a log fence,
clapping over oysters into the channel
on white mares, on the backs of white mares.

Worm Truth

Neighbors scorn an unkempt lot
Where I go down to rest
In grasses tall, tasseled out,
Where worms beneath my chest

Whisper truths of former lives
Spent long before I came,
Just waiting here to have my ear
Pressed closely to their claim,

To their regrets and epitaphs:
That they had not, in turn,
Come here to rest and contemplate
To hear their fathers yearn

For things they'd seldom spoke,
Tell the burdens of their years,
Because they too had never paused
In the vacant grass of fears,

Where worms that feed on sorrow
speak mysteries to patient ears.

Solution for Bed Bugs
for Alex

Spray your bed
with a mix of water and pine sol.
They hate the stuff.
You'll sleep wet for awhile
but they won't bug you the whole night
except for one or two survivors.

> The devil comes
> like a thief in the night.
> First you lose your rest
> and then your mind.

One time I was sitting in my chair
and a big one landed right beside me.
I dropped him in a bowl of my solution
and watched him sink to the bottom
straight to hell. Oh, did that feel good.

Contemplative Theology

Contemplation at its best happens
by a warm surprise of grace
in the seminary library,
bone dry and boxed in by book shelves
systematically theologized,
when light patterns play on the grassy slope
outside the window
a single row of cherry trees on its crest
brushed by a whisper of wind dancing light down.

Search for a name to give it:
Waterfall of Cherry Light? Dappled Down of Heaven?
Labels elude the euphoric glory.
But all states of mystical bliss
face a theological conundrum
when heaven meets the contingencies of *terra firma*.

Like now, floating gently down the slope
a transparent piece of rubber the shape of a penis
flattens against the clean seminary glass pane,
redacting your contemplative vision.

So you have to conjure new names for bliss:
*A Prick in Paradise? Now we see
through a glass darkly?*
But neither diction suits
this intercepting contraceptive,
this dick of a contradiction,
any more than your majestic mystery itself
will fit into a flattened rubber.

Afterglow

After the fireworks,
the oo's and ah's, the applause,
the cheers,
after the smoke clears
gunpowder still lingers
like the untimely fart of a lover.

And up through the clouds
in the afterglow,
there's a wink from the moon who watches
all this time as usual with the above-view.
She beams down

a casual remark to those played out
and retiring early home:
Is that all you've got? she teases,
wooing the stout but tender hearted to tarry longer
in her amorous chambers under the stars
and lie wondering up in late reverie,
hands and legs splaying
all our confessions and dreams
laid bare.

Heaven By the Back Door

At the back of bus nine
the prophet in ratty blue jeans
prattles on about U.F.O.'s
and the aliens who took him aboard:
      bright lights,
      floating beds through trees
      and surgical work.
He shakes his tangled beard
to the woman in business suit and heels
who obliges with glances
at his sandaled feet, at his bony fingers
playing the air like a flute.

She gropes for the bell chord, for a way off
this trip, when a word from him
audible only to her,
both benign and beguiling,
ignites something
she may have dreamed once
in the hallow of a flower bed,
or may have hoped
while plucking white sheets
out of a blue June, her hand
raised like a prayer on the line.

Then the probing utterance
is gone like a bird from a wire
as the bus doors fold open.
She rises glancing at the prophet

with an unwitting glint of her pearly whites
as she cracks the door of paradise
and squeezes through.

Reincarnation

this Wednesday
in the West End
we are

one
slow-moving wave
of drum-toting and golden-castanets-clinging
I-wanna-be-a-Hari-Krishna's
and oooo
don't I look cool
just floatin' down Davie here
(if Dad could see me now)
in my free-flowing saffron robe and
wax   chrome   dome

beats so-called home   beats school
beats used needles   and cold pavement
panning lonely quarters

this slow blazing like
one gorgeous orange flame
through condo heaven   in West End
with my new   found   friends
looking   for somewhere
to   burn   out

to the sea maybe
yes   all the way
down to the sweet sea

and don't stop   no   don't stop now
until we
are all   gone   out
into the deep wide blue

until I am   everything
and no thing
but a saffron lotus on the waves
washing up onto Kits beach
another Wednesday
for some poor soul
like a dog maybe
to pick up   and run   to

Flamenco

She stands statuesque,
hands on hips, gazing down
steely-eyed as Cleopatra
on her waiting subjects.
One hand extends slowly up,
the other follows,
grasping the first. Fire.

The blaze trembles down
the length of her legs,
snaps and ignites
the timbre of feet and hardwood.

Her fingers snap overhead
as she turns and turns,
setting the silence aflame
in a whirl of flamenco viva,
her watchers caught up
in her chariot of fire.

Across the table
your hair, your eyes too,
are caught
in the blaze of visitation,
finally at rest, translated.

Vancouver Snow Day

some winter days
    simply a snowfall sets off stride
the somnambulant pace
    of a populace
treading the edge of Pacific mist

and only the full moon
    crowing through cracks
in an Igmar Bergman seascape
    can wake the walking dead

can wash out the grip of anesthetic
    solstice drip
cool prelude to a trace
    of snowbound grace
for one sanguine, zero-hovering day
    until dreams adjourn
to the slush of Pacific sleep

Winter Blast

Christmas eve as the sun drowns
in a glass of hot cider spiked
with light and old stories,
the windows gust-blast like does tensing
at a hunter's breath;
icicles tremble, and fall.

Under the tree a cricket scratches from the crèche,
feeling news of an early summer in his feet:
something burns at the icy core of winter.

Another blast coaxes dying coals;
auroras shimmer along cedar bows
that tap at a sill somewhere over head.
It pries at a latch and drafts down
the throat of stairs, descends onto gum boots
puddling by the back door, and laps up
cold shadows in empty sleeves and mitts;
from his sleep a child murmurs

for this you were born: a warm blast
descending, roaring
at the threshold of midnight
to wake crèche-borne crickets.

Moon Salts for the Homeless

The moon's translucent hue
spills blue across Kitsilano Park
between highbrow homes
and new-flung condos waiting release
from their curtained scaffolding.

Ancestors back to Abraham
bathed as I do, in moon salts
from the same high cupboard,
mind-salve for nomads,

old family remedy for this
odd Kitsilano home, where I
may buy one day
but never own as in the soul,
as with the heart,
may reside in but never live,
never walk or truly love in,

unless a Saturday moon rising
offers a reprieve
from grids of scaffolding
to come immerse in moon salts
poured as a baptism
over places called foreign,
over this Kitsilano sod,
to soak in the belonging
with my homeless fathers.

When A Prophet Is Not Welcome

To the north beyond our walking grey suits,
beyond the bay, overcast skies
are finally flung back for a window of sun
that accents a peak there.
Light slips down her fir-wooded shawl,
revealing granite shoulders,
a rounded bust. And scars from the tireless
work of excavators' backhoes,
and the pock marks of condo tracks.
Claimed, discarded, and reclaimed
like a back alley whore, she stands resilient.

Scars and fir needles on distant hills
can prick a heart gone numb, can
quicken like prophets where
manicured gardens and trees
of cultivated beauty in our town
prove forever feckless.

As if battered mountains, like the wounded,
though kept distant, will still
dispel the mist fairer when drawn close
and surprise us, reviving us
by a simple draught of ancient wood
mingled with neglect. As rivulets
of grief come coursing stone-clotted veins.
As neon flights of gulls light,
and light on their turns
over marinas of listless sails.

Acknowledgements

Some poems in this collection have previously appeared in early versions in journals including SUB TERRAIN, CRUX, and BC CHRISTIAN NEWS.

I want to thank Ralph McCall, my publisher whose enthusiasm and belief in me has pushed me to wrap up this book, which has been collecting for over a decade, into a form fit for public consumption.

I also thank The Banff Centre for the writer's oasis to regain my vision and momentum for my work. Also, my many writer friends who bore with my readings and presentations over the years in writers' groups and at literary events are invaluable to me. Their comments, incisively direct and gently honest, have helped sharpen my view to my weaknesses and strengths and thankfully to poems that should have never been.

Lastly, I thank my wife Diane for giving me the needed space to put the final touches to this collection at a time when other obligations and voices cried for attention.

LaVergne, TN USA
13 January 2011
212318LV00004B/2/P